Wombats

ABDO
Publishing Company

Big
Buddy **BOOKS**
Australian Animals

by Julie Murray

VISIT US AT
www.abdopublishing.com

Published by ABDO Publishing Company, 8000 West 78th Street, Edina, Minnesota 55439.

Copyright © 2012 by Abdo Consulting Group, Inc. International copyrights reserved in all countries. No part of this book may be reproduced in any form without written permission from the publisher. Big Buddy Books™ is a trademark and logo of ABDO Publishing Company.

Printed in the United States of America, North Mankato, Minnesota.
052011
092011

PRINTED ON RECYCLED PAPER

Coordinating Series Editor: Rochelle Baltzer
Editor: Marcia Zappa
Contributing Editors: Megan M. Gunderson, BreAnn Rumsch, Sarah Tieck
Graphic Design: Maria Hosley
Cover Photograph: *iStockphoto*: ©iStockphoto.com/keiichihiki.
Interior Photographs/Illustrations: *AnimalsAnimals - Earth Scenes*: ©Miller, Steven David (p. 21); *Getty Images*: Craig Borrow/Newspix (p. 25), Visuals Unlimited, Inc./Dave Watts (p. 19); *iStockphoto*: ©iStockphoto.com/ CraigRJD (p. 9), ©iStockphoto.com/Matejay (p. 4), ©iStockphoto.com/TimothyBall (p. 4); *Photo Researchers, Inc.*: William D. Bachman (p. 12); *Photolibrary*: Bios (pp. 7, 11, 23), Peter Arnold Images (pp. 15, 27), Photo Library (pp. 17, 27), Picture Press (pp. 7, 13, 21), Tips Italia (p. 29), WaterFrame-Underwater Images (p. 16), Wildlife (p. 5); *Shutterstock*: Robyn Butler (p. 23), Susan Flashman (p. 8); Timothy Craig Lubcke (p. 11), Rosli Othman (p. 8), tororo reaction (p. 9), Dmitriy Yakovlev (p. 9).

Library of Congress Cataloging-in-Publication Data

Murray, Julie, 1969-
  Wombats / Julie Murray.
    p. cm. -- (Australian animals)
  ISBN 978-1-61783-015-0
  1. Wombats--Juvenile literature. I. Title.
  QL737.M39M87 2012
  599.2'4--dc22
                                2011003048

Contents

Long ago, nearly all land on Earth was one big mass. About 200 million years ago, the land began to break into **continents**. One of these is an island called Australia.

Wombats live underground in homes called burrows.

Living on an island allowed Australian animals to **develop** separately from other animals. So today, many are unlike animals found anywhere else in the world! One of these animals is the wombat.

Wombat Territory

There are three types of wombats. Common wombats live in hilly forests along coasts. They are found in southeastern Australia and on the island of Tasmania.

Southern and northern hairy-nosed wombats live in grasslands and on plains. Southern hairy-nosed wombats live near Australia's southern coast. Northern hairy-nosed wombats are very uncommon. They live in a national park in central Queensland.

NORTHERN TERRITORY

QUEENSLAND

WESTERN AUSTRALIA

SOUTH AUSTRALIA

NEW SOUTH WALES

VICTORIA

TASMANIA

 Common Wombat Territory

 Southern Hairy-Nosed Wombat Territory

 Northern Hairy-Nosed Wombat Territory

Common wombats live in wet areas with lots of green plants.

Southern hairy-nosed wombats live in hotter, drier areas than common wombats.

Welcome to the Continent Down Under!

If you took a trip to where wombats live, you might find…

…wildlife sanctuaries.

Australia has many wildlife sanctuaries (SANK-chuh-wehr-ees). These areas of land are set aside to help keep uncommon plants and animals safe. Some wombats live in sanctuaries.

…cricket games.

Cricket is a sport similar to baseball. It is popular in Australia.

...eucalyptus forests.

Eucalyptus (yoo-kuh-LIHP-tuhs) trees are common in Australia. Australians call them eucalypts, gum trees, and stringybark trees. Some wombats make their homes in eucalyptus forests.

...sandy beaches.

Australia is known for its beaches. There, people enjoy water sports such as snorkeling and surfing. Wombats are also found near Australia's beaches.

Take a Closer Look

Wombats have short, thick, **muscular** bodies. They have large, flat heads with small eyes.

Most common wombats have brown fur. Their noses are bare. Most hairy-nosed wombats have grayish fur. Their noses have short, white fur.

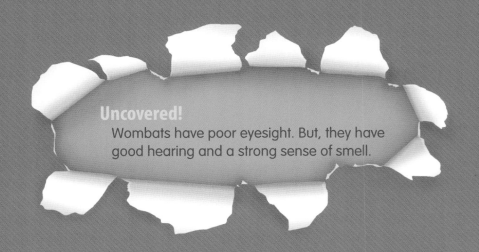

Uncovered!
Wombats have poor eyesight. But, they have good hearing and a strong sense of smell.

Hairy-nosed wombats have soft, silky fur.

Common wombats have thick fur that is not very smooth.

Wombats are big! They can be up to four feet (1.2 m) long. They can weigh up to 80 pounds (36 kg). Male wombats are usually larger than females.

A wombat has a large head for its body size.

Uncovered!
Wombats have very short tails. This helps keep them safe in their burrows. If they had long tails, predators could easily grab on and pull them out!

Wombats are sometimes called "bulldozers of the bush." They are so strong they can push through things in their way. This includes a farmer's fence!

Home Sweet Burrow

Wombats live in **burrows**. A wombat burrow is usually 10 to 100 feet (3 to 30 m) long. And, it is up to 12 feet (4 m) deep.

Some wombat burrows have several tunnels, rooms, entrances, and exits. This type of burrow is called a warren. Often, one wombat digs several warrens and smaller burrows in its home area.

Uncovered!

The size of a wombat's home area depends on how much food is available. When there is lots of food, home areas can be as small as 6 acres (2 ha). When there is little food, home areas can be larger than 60 acres (24 ha).

One wombat can have up to 30 warrens and burrows!

Built to Dig

Digging a **burrow** is hard work! Luckily, wombats are good diggers. They have strong shoulders and short, **muscular** legs. And, a wombat's feet make good shovels. They are wide with large, flat nails.

Wombats have strong mouths and sharp front teeth. These features help them cut through roots while digging.

Some wombats dig warrens as large as 650 feet (200 m) long!

A Day in the Life

Most common wombats live alone. Sometimes their home areas include shared land. But, they like to have their own places to eat and sleep. A common wombat often chases others out of its **burrows** or eating grounds. But, it allows them to visit for **mating**.

Hairy-nosed wombats are more **social**. They sometimes share a warren but sleep in different areas of it. Wombats that live together are called a mob or a colony.

Uncovered!
More than one wombat may use the same burrow but at different times.

Wombats are playful. Young wombats play fight and chase each other. They might even do somersaults!

During the day, wombats avoid the hot sun by sleeping in their **burrows**. Some sleep up to 16 hours a day! At night when it is cooler, wombats come out to search for food.

Each night, wombats spend three to eight hours searching for food and eating. During this time, they may travel more than one mile (1.6 km). They often stop at several of their burrows to dig, rest, or tidy up.

When relaxed, wombats sleep on their backs with their legs up in the air!

Wombats usually move slowly, swaying back and forth as they walk.

Mealtime

Wombats are herbivores (HUHR-buh-vawrs). This means they eat plants. Common wombats often eat grasses, roots, small bushes, and bark. Hairy-nosed wombats eat mostly grasses.

Uncovered!
A wombat's front teeth never stop growing. Eating hard plants wears them down so they don't get too long.

Common wombats sometimes search for food along coasts.

Australia's grasslands and plains are dry. So, hairy-nosed wombats have less food available than common wombats.

Baby Wombats

Wombats are part of a group of **mammals** called marsupials (mahr-SOO-pee-uhls). Marsupials have tiny babies called joeys.

Joeys are born before they are done **developing**. A newborn joey lives inside a special pouch on its mother's belly. There, it continues growing.

At three months old, a wombat joey is about the size of a human hand. But a newborn joey is as small as a jelly bean!

Female wombats usually give birth to one joey at a time. A newborn joey crawls inside its mother's pouch. There, it drinks her milk and grows.

After five to ten months, a joey comes out of its mother's pouch. But, it doesn't leave for good. For a few months after, it returns to the pouch if it senses danger. A wombat joey is ready to live on its own after 15 to 24 months.

A female wombat's pouch opens downward, toward her back legs. This helps prevent dirt from getting in as she digs. Can you see the joey in its mother's pouch?

At first, a wombat joey stays in the burrow while its mother searches for food. Later, it follows its mother around.

Survivors

Wombats face many dangers. People kill them for their fur. Farmers kill them because they harm crops. Buildings and farmland take over their **habitats**. And predators such as dingoes, foxes, and Tasmanian devils hunt them.

Still, wombats **survive**. In fact, common wombats can be found in large numbers. Wombats help make Australia an amazing place.

Wombats in the wild live for 5 to 15 years.

Uncovered!
Northern hairy-nosed wombats are one of the world's most endangered animals. This means they could die out. Scientists believe there are only about 100 left in the wild.

Crikey!
I'll bet you never knew...

...that wombat poop is cube-shaped, like dice.

...that some wombats take dust baths. These help keep their fur clean and free of bugs. To take a dust bath, a wombat lies on its side and scoops sand onto itself.

...that wombats are good swimmers.

...that the wombat's closest relative is the koala.

...that when needed, wombats can run fast! They can reach 25 miles (40 km) per hour!

Important Words

burrow an animal's underground home.

continent one of Earth's seven main land areas.

develop to go through steps of natural growth.

habitat a place where a living thing is naturally found.

mammal a member of a group of living beings. Mammals have hair or fur and make milk to feed their babies.

mate to join as a couple in order to reproduce, or have babies.

muscular (MUHS-kyuh-luhr) having strong, well-developed muscles. Muscles are body tissues, or layers of cells, that help the body move.

social (SOH-shuhl) naturally living or growing in groups.

survive to continue to live or exist.

Web Sites

To learn more about wombats, visit ABDO Publishing Company online. Web sites about wombats are featured on our Book Links page. These links are routinely monitored and updated to provide the most current information available.

www.abdopublishing.com

Index